Contents

Some words are printed in bold, **like this.** You can find out what they mean in the glossary. You can also look in the box at the bottom of the page where the word first appears.

READY FOR ACTION

Many people do activities in the mountains, such as climbing, hiking, cycling, and skiing. Mountain rescue teams save people who are hurt, lost, or **stranded** in the mountains.

Always prepared

Rescue workers must know how to **navigate** safely from place to place in dangerous **terrain**. At any given time, rescue teams could be sent on a **mission** to save someone's life.

Rescue fact!

The Vail Mountain Rescue Group is based in Vail, Colorado, in the Rocky Mountains, USA. In 2004 the group spent 1,900 hours on rescue missions. In 60 missions they saved 67 people's lives.

ATOMIC

MOUNTAIN RESCUE TEAM

JAMESON ANDERSON

Raintree

www.raintreepublishers.co.uk

Visit our website to find out more information about **Raintree** books.

To order:
☎ Phone 44 (0) 1865 888112
📄 Send a fax to 44 (0) 1865 314091
💻 Visit the Raintree bookshop at **www.raintreepublishers.co.uk** to browse our catalogue and order online.

First published in Great Britain by
Raintree, Halley Court, Jordan Hill,
Oxford OX2 8EJ, part of Harcourt
Education. Raintree is a registered
trademark of Harcourt Education Ltd.

© Harcourt Education Ltd 2007
First published in paperback in 2007.
The moral right of the proprietor has been asserted.

Editorial: Louise Galpine, Rosie Gordon,
Dave Harris, and Stig Vatland
Design: Victoria Bevan and Bigtop
Picture Research: Hannah Taylor and Sally Claxton
Production: Camilla Crask

Originated by Chroma Graphics Pte. Ltd
Printed and bound in China by WKT

10 digit ISBN 1 406 20353 X (hardback)
13 digit IBSN 978 1 406 20353 0
11 10 09 08 07
10 9 8 7 6 5 4 3 2 1

10 digit ISBN 1 406 20374 2 (paperback)
13 digit IBSN 978 1 406 20374 5
12 11 10 09 08
10 9 8 7 6 5 4 3 2 1

**British Library Cataloguing in
Publication Data**
Anderson, Jameson
Mountain Rescue Team. – (Atomic)
363.1'481
A full catalogue record for this book is available
from the British Library.

Acknowledgements

The author and publisher are grateful to the
following for permission to reproduce copyright
material: Alamy Images, pp. **9** top (Buzz Pictures),
22–23 (Robert Harding Picture Library), **26**, (Tom
Kidd), **20** bot (Ashley Cooper), **28**, (Brian Horisk),
4–5 (John Wilhelmsson/ Stockshot), **18–19**
(National Trust Photolibrary/ Joe Cornish), **10–11**,
(Shout); Corbis p. **24** top (Royalty Free); Corbis
Sygma/The Scotsman; pp. **9** bot, **16**, **27**; Corbis,
pp. **12–13** (John Van Hasselt), **6–7**, **19** inset
(Lowell Georgia); Empics, p. **24** bot (Douglas
C Pizac/AP); Science Photo Library p. **20** top
(BSIP, Platriez). Cover photograph reproduced
with permission of Alamy Images/ isifa Image
Service s.r.o.

The publishers would like to thank Diana Bentley,
Nancy Harris, and Dee Reid for their assistance in the
preparation of this book.

Every effort has been made to contact copyright holders
of any material reproduced in this book. Any omissions
will be rectified in subsequent printings if notice is given
to the publishers.

Disclaimer

All the Internet addresses (URLs) given in this book
were valid at the time of going to press. However,
due to the dynamic nature of the Internet, some
addresses may have changed, or sites may have changed
or ceased to exist since publication. While the author
and publishers regret any inconvenience this may cause
readers, no responsibility for any such changes can be
accepted by either the author or the publishers.

Sometimes the only way to reach people high in the mountains is by helicopter.

mission	task that a mountain rescue team must take part in
navigate	to get around or get through
stranded	left without a way to get out
terrain	area of land

Rescue fact!

During a blizzard in the mountains, wind can blow 160 kilometres (100 miles) per hour.

Climbers and rescuers know how to make strong knots that can hold the weight of an injured person.

What Do Rescue Teams Do?

Courageous mountain rescue teams work during avalanches, floods, mudslides, blizzards, and many other natural disasters. The rescue team might need to go to the top of a mountain or into a raging river.

Weathering the challenge

Mountain rescue workers need to be prepared for any situation. High in the mountains, the weather can change quickly. The temperature can get much colder, clouds can develop, wind can blow much more strongly, and it can start to rain or snow without much warning.

avalanche	large amount of loose snow falling down a mountain
blizzard	snowstorm with very strong winds
natural disaster	earthquake, flood, storm, or other deadly event caused by nature

How Teams Prepare

Mountain rescue workers need to train for rescue **missions**. They need to know how to use their equipment and how to work closely and safely together. Well-trained rescue workers can avoid accidents. Those who are physically fit can lift someone to safety more easily.

Knowing the land

Rescue workers also have to study the local **terrain**. Many rescue missions involve searches. By knowing the terrain, rescue workers can find a **victim** more easily. They will know the most likely places to search first.

Rescue fact!

In the USA, San Diego Mountain Rescue Team members do 20 hours of training each month.

Rescue workers may not be able to perform to the best of their ability if they do not train and are not physically fit.

victim   **person who has been harmed**

GETTING AROUND

A truck can be a mountain rescue team's most important tool. Rescue vehicles carry workers and essential equipment to a rescue scene. Rescue teams need to carry a variety of tools in their trucks, including ropes, anchors, ladders, **wetsuits**, and many other supplies.

Which trucks are used?

The trucks teams use range in size from lightweight to huge. Many rescue teams use pickup trucks with a cover on the back, which holds in their supplies. Others use command centres that are larger than a bus. They serve as offices for rescue leaders during a **mission** and hold storage cabinets and even desks.

wetsuit   **close-fitting suit of rubber worn by divers**

This jeep is designed to cope with rough ground and carry heavy loads.

IN THE AIR

Sometimes heavy snow can stop a truck. When this happens mountain rescue workers use helicopters to reach the mountain **summit**, where trucks cannot climb.

How do helicopters help in a rescue?

Rescue helicopters carry long ropes and ladders. The ladders are skillfully lowered by workers to an awaiting victim. During helicopter **missions**, rescue crews sometimes lower a **stretcher** to workers waiting on the ground. Workers at the scene of a disaster quickly and carefully place victims on the stretcher. They then signal for the crew on the helicopter to pull them up. Helicopters then take victims to rescue headquarters or a nearby hospital.

stretcher	flat, movable bed that carries a person who has been hurt
summit	top or highest peak

All helicopter crews, such as this French police rescue team, are highly trained.

GENDARMERIE

Rescue fact!

A rescue helicopter can cost around five million pounds.

Rescue Helicopter

When many mountain roads are covered with snow, helicopters can travel to places where trucks cannot go. Helicopters can make **vertical** landings and can take off from the same small location.

The pilot has to hold the helicopter steady when winching people from the ground.

vertical   straight up or down

If the weather is bad and a helicopter cannot fly, rescue workers must make the climb themselves.

Rescue fact!

The highest mountain in the world is Mount Everest in the Himalayan Mountains, between Nepal and Tibet. The mountain's summit is 8,850 metres (29,035 feet) above sea level.

Climbing Skill

Sometimes rescuers are called to help mountain climbers. Even professional mountain climbers can get stuck because of bad weather or because something fails with their equipment.

On foot

When trucks or helicopters cannot reach an area, rescue teams use their mountain-climbing skills.

Some mountain rescue **missions** can take days to complete. If a climber is **stranded** on a **remote** mountain **ledge**, only other climbers can reach them.

ledge	small surface that sticks out of a wall of rock
remote	far away from busy areas
sea level	level of the ocean, used as a starting point for measuring the height of land

HANGING ON

A sturdy rope is the most important tool for mountain climbers. Most climbing ropes are between 7 and 11 millimetres (0.3 and 0.4 inches) thick. Climbing ropes are made of slightly stretchy nylon material.

Getting to the top

Climbers carry rope with them while they climb. To make climbs at high **altitude**, climbers need lightweight equipment so they don't get weighed down and tired.

Rescue workers use **crampons** and ice picks to help support them as they climb a mountain. Crampons attach to the bottom of a climber's shoes. They have up to sixteen spikes on each foot.

altitude   height above sea level

crampons   spikes connected to a mountain climber's boots

The spikes on crampons are about 2.5 centimetres (1 inch) long.

Climbers' carabiners (loops) and ropes are very light and strong.

After they locate victims, rescue workers need to treat them right away.

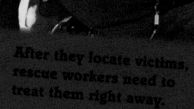

Rescue fact!

People can die from hypothermia in as little as two hours.

An immobilizer prevents causing any more damage to the spine.

MOUNTAINTOP EMERGENCY

Mountain rescue workers carry bandages and other first-aid supplies to a rescue scene. Many are also trained as paramedics.

Essential equipment

Rescue workers use a **stretcher** called an immobilizer if they think a **victim** may have a neck injury. An immobilizer keeps a victim's back and neck from moving.

Rescue teams also help people suffering from **hypothermia** or from "mountain sickness", a lack of **oxygen** in the body. Teams carry special blankets and oxygen supplies. They can help stop these dangerous conditions getting any worse.

hypothermia	condition in which a person's body temperature is very low
oxygen	gas that we need to breathe
paramedic	person trained to give emergency medical help

WHAT IS AN AVALANCHE?

An **avalanche** is an enormous amount of snow that plummets down a mountain. Avalanches start when loose snow slides. This makes more snow come loose and slide. Most avalanches travel at 100 to 130 kilometres (60 to 80 miles) per hour.

Buried

Avalanches can cause a disaster. They can cover entire climbers' camps, and sometimes even bury small towns.

Avalanche-related disasters require the help of rescue teams. However, an avalanche can also occur while a rescue team is already out on a **mission**, which makes their job even more dangerous.

Rescue fact!

The first record of an avalanche was in the Swiss Alps, a mountain range in Europe, in 1302.

An avalanche such as this one is unstoppable. In the USA, eighteen people are killed by avalanches each year.

After a large snowstorm, rescue workers can receive as many as 500 reports of avalanches in their area. They need snowmobiles to quickly get to people who need help.

BE AWARE!!
YOU ARE NOW OUTSIDE THE
SKI AREA BOUNDARY
AVALANCHE SLIDE AREA
YOU ARE ON YOUR OWN
EXTREME AVALANCHE HAZARDS
MAY EXIST
SERIOUS OR FATAL INJURIES
ARE POSSIBLE!!
CALL (970) 855-5512
KNOW THE HAZARD BEFORE YOU GO
BE RESPONSIBLE!!!

BACKCOUNTRY
ACCESS POINT
AREA BOUNDARY
EXTREME AVALANCHE
DANGER EXISTS BEYOND
THIS POINT
NO SKI PATROL
NO AVALANCHE CONTROL
YOU ARE RESPONSIBLE
FOR LEARNING ABOUT
AND AVOIDING NATURAL
HAZARDS, INCLUDING
AVALANCHES
RESCUE IS BY AUTHORITY OF
SUMMIT COUNTY SHERIFF

ATTENTION!
BACKCOUNTRY USERS
KNOW HOW TO USE
AVALANCHE BEACONS,
PROBES AND SHOVELS.
CARRY THEM AT ALL TIMES.
NEVER TRAVEL IN THE
BACKCOUNTRY ALONE.
YOU ARE RESPONSIBLE FOR
YOUR OWN ACTIONS, YOUR
OWN RESCUE, THE COST OF
YOUR RESCUE, AND WAIVE
ALL CLAIMS FOR INJURY

YOU ARE LEAVING
THE SKI RESORT
YOU CAN
DIE
THIS IS YOUR DECISION

118

Skiers are warned not to ski in areas that are likely to have avalanches.

DEEP SNOW RESCUE

Rescue workers keep watch where they think **avalanches** might occur. They monitor mountain slopes for build up of snow and ice.

Keeping track of skiers

Skiers and snowboarders are at risk of being caught in avalanches. Rescue workers sometimes keep track of how many people are in **remote** mountain areas so that they know where to look for victims if an avalanche occurs.

Rescue fact!

A completely buried avalanche victim can die within 25 minutes.

DIGGING FOR SURVIVORS

Rescue teams use shovels to dig for victims after an avalanche. They also use probes, which are long poles they poke into the snow to feel for bodies.

How can dogs help?

Rescue teams also use dogs. Dogs can sniff and find the scent of a human buried under snow. A well-trained dog team can investigate 1 hectare (2.5 acres) of land in about 30 minutes. It would take twenty rescue workers several hours to search the same area.

Dogs are valuable rescue team members.

Rescue fact!

Sixty-five percent of people living in Switzerland live in areas where avalanches are a risk. The country builds walls around some cities. It also protects its forests, which act as natural walls against avalanches.

A rescuer probes under an avalanche fall.

probe   long pole that is used to poke under the surface of snow

A rescuer warms up with a hot drink at the end of his mission.

MISSION ACCOMPLISHED

Rescue workers put in long hours at their important job. A rescue team's greatest reward is when a **mission** is successfully completed.

Rescue workers must always be prepared for their next mission.

Volunteer heroes

In most mountain communities, rescue workers volunteer their time. They are not paid for their rescue work. They volunteer to work in the rescue team because they want to save other people.

Glossary

altitude height above sea level

avalanche large amount of loose snow falling down a mountain

blizzard snowstorm with very strong winds

crampons spikes connected to a mountain climber's boots

hypothermia condition in which a person's body temperature is very low

ledge small surface that sticks out of a wall of rock

mission task that a mountain rescue team must take part in

natural disaster earthquake, flood, storm, or other deadly event caused by nature

navigate to get around or get through

oxygen gas that we need to breathe

paramedic person trained to give emergency medical help

probe long pole that is used to poke under the surface of snow

remote far away from busy areas

sea level level of the ocean, used as a starting point for measuring the height of mountains and other natural features

stranded left without a way to get out

stretcher flat, movable bed that carries a person who has been hurt

summit top or highest peak

terrain area of land

vertical straight up or down

victim person who has been harmed

wetsuit close-fitting suit of rubber worn by divers

Want to Know More?

Books

✷ *People at Work in Mountain Rescue*, Deborah Fox (Dillon, 1999)

✷ *Wilderness Search Dogs*, Daniel A. Greenberg (Bearport, 2005)

✷ *Rescues!*, Sandra Markle (Millbrook, 2006)

✷ *Rescue Dogs*, Judith Janda Presnall (Kidhaven, 2002)

Websites

✷ www.csac.org
You'll find lots of information about avalanches here.

✷ www.glencoe-mountain-rescue.com
See pictures and read stories from volunteer rescuers in Scotland.

✷ www.mra.org
Click through fun links and see pictures of the high-tech operations of many Mountain Rescue Teams.

If you liked this Atomic book, why don't you try these...?

Index

Notes for adults

Use the following questions to guide children towards identifying features of explanation text:

Can you find an example of a main heading and side heading on page 8?

Can you find the different stages of a helicopter rescue on page 12?

Can you find two examples of the present tense on page 18?

Can you give an example of a connective from page 22?

Can you give examples of side headings starting with 'how' and 'which'?